King Burue
changes the rules

by Natalija Bajlo

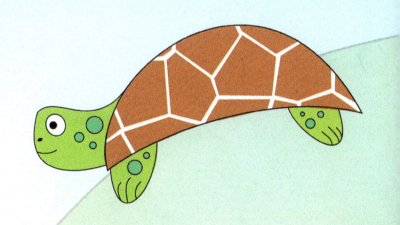

illustrated by Amene Beheshti

KING BURUE CHANGES THE RULES

By Natalija Bajlo
Illustrated by Amene Beheshti

Published by Bajlo Innovative Enterprises
www.kingburue.com

Copyright ©2014 Natalija Bajlo
ISBN 978-1-62840-492-0
Library of Congress Number 2014935271

All rights reserved. No part of this book may be reproduced or transmitted in any form or by any means electronic or mechanical, including photocopying, recording or by any information storage and retrieval system without written permission from the publisher.

Editorial, Production Coordination, Publicity
The Sayles Organization, Woodland Hills, California
www.saylesorganization.com

Book design by: Marion Redmond
Redmond and Associates,
Los Angeles, California
www.marioncreative.com

Printed in the U.S.A

Dedicated to my MOM,

who cares for me and loves me more than anything.

I love you.

In memory of my Aunt Natalija,

who watches over us.

And special thanks to the best teacher ever,

Mrs. Michelle Neuhaus, for teaching me how to write.

Love,

Natalija

Once upon a time...

there lived a goose named Burue. He was the King and protector of the Kingdom of Kalos and all the animals loved him. He was a very smart goose and he did all the right things by following the rules.

The rules were simple and seemed easy to follow.

They were made a long time ago by a very, very, very old and wise goose.

Rule #1
Tell the truth.

Rule #2
Be kind

Rule #3
Share

Rule #4
A goose can only marry a goose

King Burue liked to fly. He would think a lot in the sky. One day when he was out flying around above the green fields, he met a Japanese parrot named Kimiko. It was love at first sight, so King Burue asked Kimiko to marry him. He was so happy and it seemed like the right thing to do.

But now the King had a problem. He broke a rule. A big rule. A very old rule that had never been broken ever before. Poor Burue, even though he was not hurting anyone, he couldn't forget that he was the King and he could not break the oldest, biggest rule in the Goose Kingdom. So instead, the very happy goose thought of a plan.

"Ah-ha!" exclaimed King Burue to Kimiko. " I will disguise you to look like a goose."

The King glued white feathers to cover the parrot's beautiful bright colors. Kimiko did not seem to mind because she was so happy to be with Burue. He even taught her how to swim, but when Kimiko got in the pond, the silky white goose feathers began to fall off in the water. King Burue looked at her hopelessly!

King Burue had to think, so he told Kimiko he would go fly around and come up with a plan. When Burue said goodbye to Kimiko, she began to cry. "Why is this a rule?" Burue was quiet for a long time. Then he held her wing and said, "It was written a very, very, very long time ago by the oldest and wisest goose of all. So there must be a good reason." Kimiko waved goodbye as King Burue flew off.

He didn't know what to do next, so he just flew around. When Burue didn't know the answers to complicated questions like this one, he would fly.

As he flew up into the tree tops something soared across his path. It was his old friend, Eagle. "Hello, Eagle!" yelled King Burue. Eagle was looking for something and had not noticed the goose flying toward him.

"King Burue! Greetings!" Eagle pointed downward with his beak and Burue followed. They both landed in a grassy area near the water's edge.

"What brings you out so far from the kingdom, dear King?" Eagle put his massive wing around the dark feathered goose and led him toward the shore.

"I'm kind of on a journey, you could say," replied Burue.

"Really? What kind of journey?" asked Eagle.

The King explained that when he was stuck on a problem he would fly so that he could think.

He wasn't sure what he was looking for, but he knew he would find the answers if he kept looking for them.

Then he asked Eagle, "Hmmm...tell me, Eagle, have you ever liked someone that wasn't an eagle?" Eagle didn't answer and continued walking to the water. There on a large rock was a medium-sized pelican, who was scooping fish out of the sea and laying them neatly on the shore.

"Perhaps you should meet my companion, Pelican."

"Pelican, we have a stranger in town!" Eagle shouted.

Pelican looked up with disbelief and bowed.

"Oh please, get up, get up. I really dislike that King stuff," said King Burue, almost seeming annoyed.

"But I bow to show my respect, dear King," Pelican said, smiling. So King Burue bowed back, "And I bow to show my respect as well." Then they both giggled.

Pelican kindly offered a fish to Eagle and to King Burue.

"You see," said Eagle after he ate his fish, "Pelican found me helpless with a broken wing. I couldn't get food. He helped me heal and brought me fish to get strong again."

"I see," said the King, "That is amazing kindness."

Pelican smiled. "I admire Eagle. He has taught me that being different on the outside doesn't mean that we are that different on the inside."

Just then, an overwhelmed porcupine came wobbling down the path as fast as his little legs could go. "Pelican, Eagle, can you please help?" he yelled loudly.

They all ran toward Porcupine quickly. "Please help," Porcupine barely said. He was so out of breath, he couldn't talk anymore. A golden yellow bunny hopped up behind him. "Oh, he's just overreacting," she said calmly. "Porcupine is so nervous about those silly quills." Bunny turned around and there was a long quill stuck next to her cute bunny tail.

"Ouch!" said King Burue. "Let me help you, Bunny."

Porcupine couldn't look. King Burue pulled out the quill.

Pelican covered his eyes too.

"See, it was nothing at all," said Bunny.

"How did that happen?" asked Eagle.

Bunny smiled. "Porcupine never thought he would ever be able to hug because of his sharp quills." Porcupine got excited. "But Bunny showed me how I can be soft just like she is and now I can hug all the time!" Just then, Porcupine's quills went straight up and everyone jumped back.

"Oops! So sorry!" he said, blushing. "We're still working on when he gets too excited," laughed Bunny.

"I've seen such beautiful acts of kindness and sharing. Thank you all for telling me your stories," the King said.

Eagle and Pelican bowed to the King. Bunny wiggled her nose and her whiskers and Porcupine waved. King Burue flew off.

King Burue was getting thirsty so he stopped at a pond to get a drink of water. There he met a frog.

"Are you the King?" asked the frog.

"Of course he is. How many geese have you seen wearing a crown?" said another voice that seemed like it was coming from the frog.

The king looked puzzled. "I'm sorry, Frog. That seemed like it came from you, but it's not the same voice."

"I cannot lie, my King," said the second voice, but it was not the frog. A chameleon suddenly stuck its head up from behind the frog's back. They were both a pretty green.

The frog made a croaking sound and said, "Oh dear. You've done it now."

The chameleon changed colors to a pretty purple when she moved from the frog's back to a flower on a lily pad.

"We're tired of hiding."

"Hiding from whom?" questioned King Burue.

The chameleon paused and said, "From you. From everyone."

"But why would you hide?" he asked.

"It's the last rule," croaked the frog.

The chameleon continued speaking. "Is it not clear that I am a chameleon and my friend is a frog?" she asked.

"We share everything. She is kind and honest and most of all we are happy together."

King Burue looked deep in thought. Ah-ha. A goose shall only marry a goose, the King recalled. A frog shall only marry a frog. A chameleon shall only marry a chameleon. A bunny shall only marry a bunny. A porcupine shall only marry a porcupine. A pelican shall only marry a pelican and an eagle shall only marry an eagle.

"Yes, you are right," said the King.

"That is the last rule." King Burue was thinking about all that he saw on his journey.

"Thank you, friends," said the King as he flew off.

King Burue came to the cave. He yelled into it.

"Grandpapa!" he called.

Slowly, a very old goose came to the light. They hugged.

"What brings you here, my great-grandson?"

King Burue looked serious. "You are a very old and wise goose. Before you, a very, very, very old and wise goose made the rules a very, very, very long time ago."

"Yes, this is true."

"The first three rules make good sense. They are simple things that remind us how to be good to one another," Burue said. "But Grandpapa, I have traveled and seen with my own eyes that there is no reason for the last rule."

The old goose nodded his head up and down. "I am proud of you, Burue," he said. "You saw that kindness, honesty and happiness are not found in the color of your feather or your fur. It doesn't matter what you look like. A rule can't tell you about your heart."

"So there is really no reason for that rule, Grandpapa?" Burue asked. A flamingo came out from the cave and curled her long neck up around Grandpapa. He smiled.

"No reason at all, Burue. Remember, the most important rule is the first one. Tell the truth and the rest of the rules are easy."

"Thank you, Grandpapa."

King Burue flew back to Kimiko. He hugged her and told her all about his journey. She looked happy.

The next day, the entire kingdom was gathered outside the castle. King Burue came out to speak to them.

"The idea of the rules is a way to remind us of the important things about how to treat one another," the King said. "Some rules are made without having a lot of information and don't make sense at all." The crowd is quiet. They don't seem to understand.

King Burue looked into the crowd. "Eagle, you told me an amazing story about kindness with Pelican. Bunny, you shared a valuable lesson with Porcupine and gave him an endless gift, and Chameleon, you and Frog told the truth, which makes everything quite clear.

"And you..." Burue said, looking at his elder.

Grandpapa came forward with Flamingo on his arm.

"Yes, you, Grandpapa, taught me that rules can be changed when they don't work."

Kimiko stepped out next to King Burue. He smiled.

"You can't help who you are and you can't help if you like someone who isn't a goose."

The crowd cheered and King Burue and Kimiko lived happily ever after...and so did all of his friends.

"The idea of the rules is a way to remind us of the important things about how to treat one another."
– King Burue

What rules do you follow?

Eight-Year-Old Child Changing the World...
One Story at a Time

King Burue Changes the Rules is a children's story with an adult dilemma told so simply through the keen interpretation of an eight-year-old child. The theme is one of diversity that goes a step further with a lesson about embracing who you are while accepting others in the same way. It is not uncommon and, yet, still a challenge, leading children to believe they have to fit a "norm" designated by invisible rules, instead of celebrating individuality. The delicate boundaries of diversity are revealed using animals and told in a way that is so rich in context.

Natalija Tatjana Bajlo, the author, is a young gifted child who has a very mature perspective with untainted notions. Her fable exemplifies the mantra of acceptance accompanied by the rules of trust, kindness, selflessness and the need to be true to your heart. A goose, who defies his own kingdom's rule when he marries the lovely Japanese parrot, Kimiko, attempts to disguise her as one of his own kind by covering up her unique beauty. The plan falls apart and the King sets off on a journey to find a solution.

He unexpectedly discovers that all he once believed to be right, based on a rule made up a long, long time ago, was actually quite wrong. When King Burue witnesses how his friends had found solace in the companionship of unlikely mates, it leads him to challenge the tradition of many generations when he proposes to change the rules.

The illustrator, Amene Beheshti, adds another unique dimension that flourishes with the imagination of the writer and truly makes it a modern day allegory, with a lesson for the parent as well.

Stories that fortify kindness and teach children to examine without bias will be an invaluable resource for social development. A vehicle for parents to teach their children that it doesn't matter what we look like, but instead, what defines us is how we treat others and contribute as a person, this story raises the consciousness of self-awareness as it relates to how we affect others. Building self-esteem while breaking down the barriers between people lessens the motive of hate and, hopefully, will reduce bullying as these children grow up being intrigued by their differences rather than fearing them. Making changes for tomorrow begins early in life.

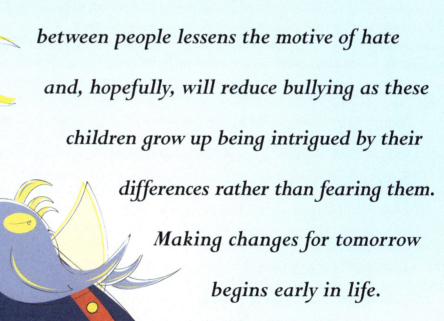

"A child relays the challenges of diversity within a storybook with the hopes of teaching other children to love more and hate less."

Natalija Bajlo, eight-year-old author of *King Burue Changes the Rules*, is an extraordinary young lady who is very observant of the world around her. It is with an open heart that she adamantly delivers her message based on how she was taught to treat others. When Natalija is faced with issues at school where kids seem to act quickly to ridicule others, she does the opposite and speaks out on behalf of the one being challenged. The true beauty in her refusal to see the differences in people lends itself to seeing more of the uniqueness in them instead.

A creatively active mind sets the stage for Natalija's book. She writes with a purpose around which her narrative skillfully evolves. She will tell you that other "morals" arise as the story unravels, such as the idea of being able to love who you love regardless of what "rules" may try to condemn your union. That's why you should never disguise your own beauty just to fit in nor should you fear or hate what is different just because you were told to do so, Natalija says. Instinct compels her to voice her opinions, which is what she displays through King Burue's need to change a rule that was made for no apparent reason at all. "You don't know how to hate unless somebody teaches you to hate" is what she says about obstacles of diversity. Inspired by the great messages of Dr. Martin Luther King, Jr., Natalija especially takes to heart his famous quote, "…they will not be judged by the color of their skin, but by the content of their character," and uses the word "color" in her story to represent all perceived differences between the characters.

We are most thankful for the amazing teachers in the Los Angeles Unified School District. Natalija has been fortunate to have had the very best mentors teaching her how to write and encouraging her talent for storytelling. She is already working on her next fable with hope that her words will be not only enjoyable but will help children put an end to prejudice on many levels maybe just by learning to be kinder to one another.

Illustrator Amene Beheshti, is quite a unique and talented young lady. Born in the Persian province of Qom in 1986, Amene was in love with colors and colorful pencils ever since she created her first drawing. She received her degree in painting from Iran's Isfahan Art University in September, 2013. Now, Amene works as an illustrator and shows her feelings via her illustrations. When she had the opportunity to read Natalija's book, Amene felt an instant connection to the meaning of the story that served as inspiration for her delightful drawings of the characters and the world in which they live. Children will be enthralled with the messages in her illustrations and how playful they are with such a creative twist. Amene has many great visual stories to tell through her art. We anticipate seeing much more of her in the near future and look forward to more collaborations.

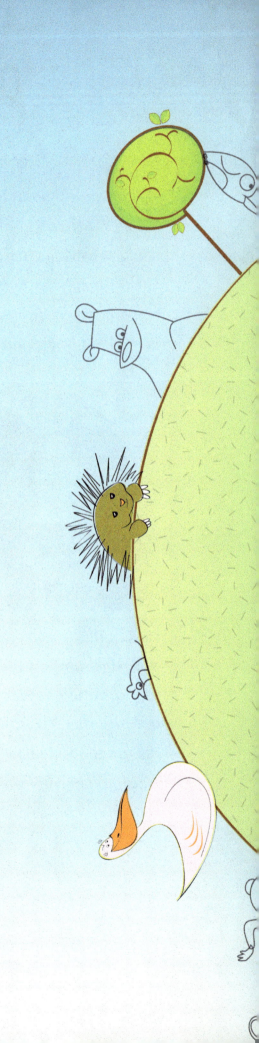

Acknowledgments

Our sincere appreciation to the amazing friends who helped make this book a reality. Thank you for believing in us!

Kelly and Steve Bailo	Vanessa McCullers
Jadranka Bajlo	Jazzie McCullers
Sime Bajlo	Alissa Neubauer
Susan Bailo	Mary Neubauer
Baba Tatjana	Scott Neubauer
Bonnie Brosnahan	Michelle Neuhaus
Max Bruni	Bethany C. Putnam
Barbara Blackburn	Holly Root
Debbie Cane	Sandor–Pitcher Clan
Chandra Galasso	Peggy & Lee Scroggins
Kelly Gordon	Molly Snow
Janet & Joel Johnson	Mike Starr
Matt Helliwell	Christy Sumner
Mayre Martinez	Les Williams
Kristi McEnvoy	Elad Yifrach
Merrill Moore	

CPSIA information can be obtained
at www.ICGtesting.com
Printed in the USA
LVOW06*2332110517
534238LV00034B/797/P